Book of Parables II

Divine Lessons #17-35 from "Thy Kingdom Come"

BRIAN SMITH

Copyright © 2018 by Brian Smith, DDS Publishing

1st Edition

This is a work of fiction. Names, characters, places and incidents are either the product of the author's imagination or are used fictionally. Any resemblance to actual persons or organizations, living or dead, is entirely coincidental.

No part of this book may be reproduced in any manner whatsoever without written permission, except in the case of brief quotations embodied in the critical articles and reviews.

Printed and bound in the USA.

Cover design, symbols, characters, names, music, artwork, interior layout, are film protected.

ISBN: 978-0-9991641-4-3

*"Ye shall know the truth,
and the truth shall make you free."*
John 8:32

Introduction

Book of Parables II is the fifth book written in the series "Thy Kingdom Come". This book was written to be a companion aid to your personal Bible study and growth. The series was not written to take the place, nor over-shadow, nor lessen any of parabolic messages taught by our Lord Jesus Christ. Only He can teach true parables, forgive personal sin, purify the soul, perform heavenly miracles, heal the sick, and also raise Himself from the dead. No mortal can do any these things, only He can.

This book was written using biblical scripture with the intention to bring additional emphasis to the lost vs. broken, the saved vs. the unsaved, and to all who have not sought in earnest the wisdom and enlightenment from the Parables which Jesus Christ taught. May you, the reader, receive many blessings from the Book of Parables II, inspired from the wisdom and teachings of the Holy Scriptures, which will bring you closer to eternal salvation, forgiveness, peace, happiness, and joy; also, that you also might better walk in God's Light forever, and inherit Eternal Life under His care with His boundless love, grace, mercy and hope ever-lasting...

Jesus said…

"What is highly valued among men,
is detestable in God's sight."

Luke 16:15

Book of Parables II (17-35)

The Parable of Man's Season of Circles 1

The Parable of God's Hand vs. Man's Hand 4

The Parable of God's Invisible vs. Man's Visible........................7

The Parable of Man's Inhumanity toward Man 11

The Parable of the Weaving of Man's Soul 14

The Parable of Man's Self-Destruction 17

The Parable of One Who Listened 19

The Parable of Man's False Idols...21

The Parable of Man's Secret Treasure 23

The Parable of Man's Injustice to Man 25

The Parable of Man's Force of Reason................................29

The Parable of The Red Cape 32

The Parable of The Need for Judas 34

The Parable of The Bastard World 36

The Parable of The Lost and Found....................................38

The Parable of The Blessing, The Fruit, and The Treat 41

The Parable of the Tithe..43

The Parable of the Wicked, the Worrisome, and the Proud 44

Divine Lesson: #17

The Parable of Man's Season of Circles

A dead man walking whose name still remains unknown went before the Lord and asked, "How do I measure myself that I might gain entrance into the Kingdom of Heaven?" The Lord said to him, "Sell all that you have, give the money to the poor, and then follow me?"[1]

Then the man said to the Lord, "Tell me, then, how do I measure these things, for I do not know… I am not smart in these ways!"

"Then the Lord God said to this man, "I tell you the truth. My thoughts are not your thoughts, and My ways are not your ways.[2] My words, unlike your words, can-not spun to have dual meanings, or made to be spoken in circles. Man speaks out of both sides of his mouth, but I do not. Listen closely…This is the way of the world of Satan. Do you not understand this? If you love your parents or your children more than Me, then you are not worthy of Me[3]; yet you still cling to the things of the world in which you live; and all these things have multiple meanings. All

---

[1] Luke 18:22
[2] Isaiah 55:8-9
[3] Matthew 10: 37

-- Book of Parables II --

things of the lower world were created to exist in circles which I created to remain steady. In order to break these circles, and enter into My Kingdom, you must leave the circles of your life, and not love anything of the lower world more than Me.[4] For all material things… those things which you are able to touch, collect, taste, and breath will dearly pass away from you and be kept in the circles of Lower Paradise; but My love and My grace is enough for you surely, for it, nor I will never pass away.[5] It is free of all these things. For of the world, seen or unseen, large are small, living or non-living, these were all made by Me, and these are Mine, for they belong to no other; and they will not pass from this world with you or without you, because they exist in circles.

People and their governments, they will wage war on each other to try to win others from Me, the Devil will try to take them from Me, while man will try to hide[6] them from Me, but none shall ever succeed… These things of the world I loan only temporarily for mankind to use all for my glory, and then will I run them back to Me ashore. I tell you truly… Can you really hope to control the oceans, the skies, the mountains, or the cosmos? No! They are only on My loan for use by My Living Word…

For everything which I created, there is a season, for man in his world, both good and bad, each in its own epoch, boding his time, one followed by another until I renew all things according to My will. You, my children, will pass from one season to the next and live and die in circles, lest you claim Me as yours, and break out of them. But first, just as you were born from the dust, you must be born of

---

[4] I Corinthians 13:3
[5] John 3:16
[6] Revelation 6:16

the Spirit. Your purpose is but a test, and a journey of faith, Holy or not, and known to all or not. It is a fight given to you for your eternal salvation, not an excuse for hate and worldly destruction. To this world I sent My Son, and these things to rule: the four seasons, until I come again. To many of the blessed I give more of everything…which is today, tomorrow and forever; only if they can just follow my example and be obedient.

And when you ask the your score of your test, my friend, you will not find it written in the Book of Life, lest you put your heart into Mine and take up the cross and lay it upon your back;[7] for only then, will you know all answers you seek by following Me. I tell you the truth, whoever shall lose his life for Me shall gain it, and whoever shall try to gain it for his own sake without bearing My cross, he shall lose it.[8]"

---

[7] Revelation 6:16
[8] Isaiah 64:6

-- Book of Parables II --

Divine Lesson: #18

The Parable of God's Hand vs. Man's Hand

An angel sat before the Lord's hands as the Lord counted His sheep which He had lost to distractions. The angel looked up at The Lord God Almighty and asked this question, "Oh, Lord, Creator of Heaven and Earth, and also man and angels, what separates us, the angels, from mankind this day? Why is man so burdened and lost, and we are not? He claims he is great, but woe is he, for his deeds are nothing more than soiled rags thrown at Your Feet."[9]

Then God, The Father, Creator and Deliverer, bemoaned this answer, for in all His Majesty, and for all time, He replied, "You have seen Me, and you have also traveled with Me through my Heavens, but still you ask this rank-in-file question? Do you not remember the fate of the giant named Goliath, and also the fate of his mighty army?[10] What has changed from then? Remember the man called Barabbas[11] whose name was shouted out over My Own for unearned freedom? He received only a temporary pass. My hands have always been at work before you, and they have never been tied and then are idle....I have said even to My Own Hands that always; even after they finished sorting, and sifting, and

---

[9] Isaiah 64:6
[10] I Samuel 17
[11] Matthew 27:21

making the true foundation of the church for My people on which My capstone shall be placed, that they continue to work as you must do.[12] Man, himself will wither like the rose if he has no sun, no warmth, no will,[13] and no heir; and also if he does not work. My hands are always working for him; they are never idle, and my breath which is all powerful continually breathes on him. Man's hands are never full, and his breath is as weak as a summer rain which falls only each other's ears. For I collected him out from of the ground[14] to make him into My Image, [15] and gave him two hands for praise[16] and to lift high into the sky, but back unto the ground his hands will return along with his body attached[17], lest he first becomes My flask, a clay vessel from which the Holy Spirit can be poured out[18] in My name. I have made him from a soil which once was unfertile ground, to beat him into a useful form, to be fruitful and to multiply[19], to make round his rough edges enough to make him worthy in my sight and to touch with ease; so, then to hold close in thy bosom.[20] I have emptied his insides out[21] from selfishness and from gain that he might be filled by My own measure, and put a fire under his feet that his clay vase would be made hard to last. Oh yea, I have taken the heat from My kiln and made just warm enough that it does not crack his outer shell nor break him during his cure.[22] And, because his outside will not be

---

[12] Zachariah 4
[13] Ephesians 5:5
[14] Genesis 2:7
[15] Genesis 1:27
[16] Psalm 134:2
[17] Psalm 134:2
[18] Romans 5:5
[19] Genesis 1:28
[20] Genesis 1:28
[21] Matthew 23:26
[22] Matthew 23:26

adorned while he is being taught, then I will paint on him an inside of gold in his heart the path and way of eternal life. Then after his heart is made pure, onto his outward skin so that all might see, I will bind onto him a fusion of many Eternal Hues, putting him back into the fire of the kiln once more to make My life stick onto him and with him. For this reason, he was born to be chosen: to be taken twice through the fire of formation (and maybe more for the most Holy), so he can be free from the Grip of Hades for ever more, and he can lift up his hands to praise me for his Eternal Love, that I might see him in the lose we both share which was made pure for My delivery, carried by My angels, and with the salvation bought with My blood, so that whoever then shall believe in Him, shall not perish but have everlasting life."[23]   Amen

---

[23] John 3:16

-- Brian Smith --

Divine Lesson: #19

The Parable of God's Invisible vs. Man's Visible

The Lord God looked down before his creation and said to His angels, "They shall see me only when I allow them to, and through the invisible, they shall know My Heart, and I shall know theirs." [24]

Then He said unto them all which He saw there, and also He said to those He did not see yet, "Behold for I give you myself, and I also give to you the land, the water, those that fly and those that swim, the animals of the air, and fish of the sea, all that is in it, the rain which will cleanse your dirt away, and the sun to warm your seed, but you are not to seek unto the Tree of Knowledge."[25]

Then the Lord said to those He could see, and to those He could not see, "Man will be like the land I create, renewing itself like blowing wind and desert storms.[26] His body will be like clay, whose shards will return to the land after I am done with him, [27] and his soul will be like the great ocean which needs to be tamed

---

[24] Exodus 33:12-24
[25] Genesis 2:17
[26] Ecclesiastes 3: 19-20
[27] Genesis 3:19

or the great river which needs to be dammed. He will have two main fluids which will flow from his body, just as the waters which split Eden into two halves. Man and his only soul-mate, woman, shall bring forth milk which began as stems from the ground which I produced, to nourish him and his children, a product of the seed of all seeds which I have sent, and have planted, and to which he will return[28]; then also this man and his woman shall produce their body's urine which is their by by-product, a garbage that which bring stench upon the earth, which fouls the ground he stands upon, and which pollutes the water which he shall eventually drink if he is careless in his ways.[29] I shall make all this to and from him separated from the tree of knowledge of good and evil, for when he eats from it he will surely die.[30] So that only in the invisible world, he will know Me and know My ways in his heart; and in the visible world, he will turn from Me when I stand before him because he can-not see Me. And because of these things, he will suffer all the days of his life in his mortality,[31] and he will constantly choose the visible over the invisible, seeking more of the Tree of Knowledge, only to become more lost in its legend than found in Me. I tell you the truth, for only the man who can doubt his own being, can he put his hands in my wounds and know that I walk among you,[32] and will he understand the true meaning of life, and find everlasting joy." Amen

Then one, who lived among the angels in Upper Paradise, stood up and asked if He could be a legal questioner (a proxy) for the answers He did not know. His name was Gadreel.[33] Then, and the ground shook, and the skies opened and they all looked down

---

[28] I Peter 2:2
[29] Ezekiel 21:7
[30] Genesis 2:17
[31] I Peter 3:14
[32] John 20:27
[33] Book of Enoch 69:6

over the earth. God said to this low being, "Do you not know my man? How many answers and how much land does he really need?"

Then the angel said to the Lord, "He needs only enough to have another statue to his other gods, or enough to build his foundation for another edifice to another." Then the Lord saith, and the Lord replied, "And then what?....Does he not need the land I made for him to grow his food? Does he forget my scriptures[34] of his brothers Cain and Able? Does he not need the soil to hold his waste and purify his soul? Did I his Lord not give him all that he needed, even in his suffering to need he above all?"

The angel Gadreel said, "He needs his buildings, his statutes, his coliseums, his arenas, his stages, his toys, his pride, his fun, as well as his pyramids and his condominiums, for he loves these things that makes him smile, and all that he can make with his two hands for his own glory, and his mind to give him good thoughts. He will always surely choose concrete over grass."

Then the Lord God said, "Then I will harden his heart like the concrete of his pleasures and turn his life into pillars of dead stone, like the basalt of the earth's core. I will curse him who knows not My ways, along with Gadreel, and his followers of the night, for you have questioned my Holy motives, by putting other loves before My own. So, he with you, Gadreel, shall move like ants and vipers all the days I grant them time on the earth. And then the man who follows only lies and your lead, will toil the ground under the Lordship of heat of the sun and he find no pleasure in his hoe; and the woman who follows this man shall feel the sting of childbirth then floating like a cork on the ocean in her lostness she will forget the reason I put her here to help the lost man of Adam, and to teach her children to know My Son like Mary. here I say, said and saith

---

[34] Matthew 21:42, 22:29, 26:54

-- Book of Parables II --

to you all who can hear my voice, yea, all man from this forward will need only enough land to harvest their needs which is to cover his head once he has fallen from grace, and then enough land to feed his own mouth with family to nourish, lest he leads them in the wrong ways of the wide path, that they should suffer with wars, plagues and disease. He and you must not use words nor actions to defile the land which I give him: for if then he uses My name and spurns My grace in vain, then I shall no longer give to him the land, nor sea, nor air, nor a life of joy to have dominion. For then, I shall truly shun him in his callous ways, from this precious dimension which I built for him in the sky."

-- Brian Smith --

Divine Lesson: #20

The Parable of Man's Inhumanity toward Man

There was a man who was born onto the earth, and he was born an elitist.[35] He thought he was better than the rest of the people. He went here and there with itchy ears[36] and with a tongue which defiled his own soul. God said to him one day, "How can you sit at your own table and eat with those you despise? You take from them which is not yours and use it for your own good… Is not the breath in their lungs as good as the breath in yours?" Then, the man said to God, "But you made me with a better mind, and a better imagination, and a better ethic, is not this, the spoils of my life for being better?" Then the Lord God said to the Man, "But did I make you with a better heart?[37] For, in your heart are the keys which I paid with My blood to unlock your soul."

"And what is this…my soul?" the man asked. I can-not see it. Is it here? or there? Can I put it in a bag to store it up safely for

---

[35] Romans 2: 1-11
[36] *2 Timothy 4:3*
[37] *Genesis 6:5*

the winter? What need of it do I have, if it cannot be measured for me to use or tender?"[38]

The Lord God said, "You fool! Whatever you sow, you shall reap.[39] The harvest does not jump on the table for you just to eat it. It must be prepared, washed, handled, and cleaned. For the unclean must be must be made clean. The unclean must be removed from the clean so it will not make the clean sick, lest all will surely die."[40]

The man just stood silent before God and said nothing for he knew not what question to ask, then he said, "What are some examples of this uncleanliness that you speak?"

Then God said, "It is your inhumanity and your spite for your neighbor with whom you find fault in, that causes you to be unclean. You find him to not be worthy of your food, and your cheer, so you take from him his table, and make it your own."

The man then spoke again, and said, "I do not understand."

The Lord God said to the man, "Oh you are such a spoiled rag because you have been woven of My earthly twine that you know not the depth your uncleanliness.[41] You continue to measure all things of man, all by man's measure; and not, by Mine. Your time does not belong to you. It never has, but belongs to Me, and your fruit does not belong to you but belongs to Me, your tongue does not belong to you but belongs to me, and your riches do not belong to you but belongs to me. That which belongs to you is only your pride and your arrogance which separates you from all those who know me and I know them. When I call them, they hear My voice,[42] and you hear only the words of yourself breathing in your itchy ears. I tell you the Truth, you can-not live and sell yourself

---

[38] *Revelation 6:9*
[39] *Galatians 6:7*
[40] *Matthew 23:27*
[41] *Isaiah 64:6*
[42] *John 10: 27-28*

like a prostitute in so many small ways and still be clean in My sight. All that you lay your hands to will be taken from you and then disposed of; and you will watch from afar as you smell the fires burn your life in vain. The wicked are those who kill others in the name of righteousness, for they kill not the body but the soul. These do not use the tools of man like guns, and knives, and the tools of war, but words, and falsehoods, mis-leadings, and fear. The insidiousness of elitism is the ways of death, and in that destruction, you will see the Light of Your God calling out to you in a whisper so that all can hear in a booming voice, Look at Me! Repent, and learn fast, that you can see and hear the Lamb who was killed for you that you might have Eternal Life."[43]

---

[43] *John 1:29*

-- Book of Parables II --

Divine Lesson: #21

The Parable of the Weaving of Man's Soul

An angel stood before the Lord God and asked, "Why have you given Mankind his soul to lose, and not the angels their soul to win?"[44]

Then the Lord God replied to the angel who questioned Him, "In how many ways can man grieve in his pain and suffering, and then he wish to die mercifully, or be saved in the end, which you can-not?"

"There are at least four ways my Lord, which I have observed, which are the same ways in which you make Your winds blow," said the angel.

"Explain to them now in earnest to all, my good and faithful servant, so that others may hear what they do not know or understand," the Lord commanded.

"These four traits which are sewn onto the man's soul make him different from all others. They are to be his weakness and cause him suffering and pain; his spiritual, emotional, physical, and financial tests which the angels do not possess nor carry," replied the angel. In each of these, man can trip and fall to find a disastrous relationship which is not worthy of Your Heaven, and then his soul might be lost and locked away forever. The winds may then carry

---

[44] Matthew 16:26

him from you far, far away; so far that even the love of The Holy Spirit may no longer be on his mind."

"I am listening," saith the Lord. "Do not say, that I never listen to man nor My angels, for I hear all prayers of the yearning with repentant hearts; so that others may listen and hear as well. So then, say to those who are listening now, what you have seen as you watch the earth and the men who call out in My name there."

"Each man is made perfectly imperfect, so these four things cause him pain, in anguish, when his soul is moved any distance from You, so he might become a sheep lost from its shepherd in need and protection. You have woven his soul in unison from these four as indicators of Your measure, so he can see and be invested in your commandments to obey Your laws."

"I am still listening to your learned wisdom today, My good, and faithful servant. So, how are you so different from all other mankind? How is this possible? Are not all angels smart in upper Paradise and Man in Lower Eden?"

"First, I have not any choices to make on my own, no imperfect volitions to destroy me, so my spirit can-not wander too from far from your Holy Spirit, as did with Adam and Eve. And secondly, I have not a worldly body made of skin with bones, with physical desires. I am without a physical box like David or Samson to curse me with lust, therefore I have no impurities or sharing of my mind that I must worry about, or a body which will die of disease if I cohabit immorally or deface unholy. Thirdly, I have no thoughts of my own to blemish my mind like the great kings of Pharaoh or Herod, so I have no weeds in the garden of my mind to pluck out, creating time lost which will detour me from praising you with every moment of my life in song and action. And lastly, I have not been made to survive, to eat and sleep, to work and toil like the prophets or like Ruth, or Saul; so I have no tithe due from my purse from which I can pay from my lot, because all things that

I might give to honor thee, has been created and given to me, even to the 90 percentiles above the 10% [45] you require of all."

"You answered correct My good steward, My angel," said the Lord, "You have been a good worker for Me to watch out endlessly, and with this you have received your measure of wisdom to share; so you can now collect your wings fourthly and take them up for Heaven's greater cause. I tell you the truth today, in this epoch, no other penitence is due; that all men might watch you as you serve My Son and the Holy Spirit as well, that they see Me more clearly in My-Own-Light."

---

[45] Leviticus 27:30

-- Brian Smith --

Divine Lesson: #22

The Parable of Man's Self-Destruction

The Lord God looked over Adam as He created him from the dust, and He said, "Even the greatest among you will be frail and weak. I will put into you, a severe weakness and frailty so that you will need Me." [46]

Then Adam replied, "And why is this so? You have created the birds of the air to survive, and everything that flies, crawls, or runs to be strong and survive, so why do you create us different?"

The Lord God said, "All things were created equally, made to pass from and never be heard from again; and you are the same. You shall live and die and pass never to return, but you, you shall be measured differently while you breathe. I gave you less, not more of what you need. All others I created for them to sustain, but you shall never sustain. You shall self-destruct trying to sustain, for you will try to move yourself into me; none other tries to do that."

Then Adam said, "So you curse me to be my own enemy?"

"No," says the Lord, "I shall give you an enemy, like no other. He will be invisible, quiet, cunning, and formidable. He will be all things you can-not conquer; he is not you, and you will know him not when he is around you. Like the clouds you will try to cut

---

[46] Psalm 116: 6

with a knife, he will not cut, and like the sea you will try to smite him, he will not smite, like the wind you try to contain him, you shall not contain; and like the rain you try to stop him, you shall not stop. I have created you frail and weak against his power so that you will seek my power over him. So, do not be distracted in your pursuit of me, lest you fall pray to the bidding of the invisible, and his power. At least, you can see all things I send but you will not see him, for just as you will pass from this life and never be heard of again, so he will pass through the same door, and the two of you shall either be one with me or one with him. My way is the way of glory and life. His way is the way of self-destruction and neither of these two ways shall cross, for they are divergent all your days, even unto your last breath. If you choose him as you pass from this world of frailty and weakness, you will never be heard from again. If you choose Me in just the same way as My Father, who is only Good, your life of goodness and glory will just begin, and never end." [47]

---

[47] John 3:16-21

-- Brian Smith --

Divine Lesson: #23

The Parable of One Who Listened

A man called Guthrie by his mother, and also by the good angels in Heaven, went before the Lord and asked, "How do I measure myself that I might gain the blessing of Heaven?" The Lord said to him, "Sell all that you have, give the money to the poor, and then follow me."

Guthrie then said to the Lord, "Can you tell me? How do I measure these things?"

"Then the Lord God said to the man called Guthrie, "The word ALL, does not have dual meanings. Do you not understand? How slow are you with my words? You still cling to the world in which you live, but to enter the Kingdom of Heaven you must not own anything but that which is of Me. For all which is made by me, is mine. Governments will try to take it, the Devil will try to take it, man will try to take it, but none shall succeed… I loan only these things to them for My glory. Tell Me, do you own the oceans, the skies, the seas, and the cosmos? No! They are only on loan…For everything I have created there is a season, an epoch, one followed by another until I renew it according to my will. You too, Guthrie, will pass from one season to the next; for life is a journey, not a destination.

-- **Book of Parables II** --

To the world I set up all things accordingly, using the four seasons, until I come again, but to you, I will give many more, today, tomorrow and forever, if you follow my Words... When you ask for the answer to your destination, you will not find it lest you abide in ME and take up My cross and put upon your back; only then will you know true wisdom of the answer you seek by following Me. I tell you the truth, whoever shall lose his life for Me shall gain it, and whoever will try to gain his life without Me shall lose it. And, to this man, God's message was heard clearly. He sold all that he had, then follow Christ so he could have all that was more, and have it more pleasing and more abundantly before God."[48] Amen

---

[48] Matthew 16:25, John 10:10

-- Brian Smith --

Divine Lesson: #24

The Parable of Man's False Idols

There was a woman who loved her children and wanted them grow up in the Ways-of-The- Lord. Her name was Ann. She asked the Lord, "Good teacher, what must I do for my children to gain entrance into heaven, for they have nothing to sell, or to give to the poor as you have commanded the good to do?"

Then the Lord said, "They have no money or inheritance of their own, so, 'Who do you say that I am'? No-one is good –except God alone.[49] As your Savior, and blood of your blood, do you put before them the non-sense of putting other things before them instead of Me? What do you do on the days of My celebration of both my birth and death? What do you do all the days of My life when you find Me gone, but still near? What do you do all the days of your life when you struggle to feed your flock because they tarry, and what do you do all My days, those of which are only days of toil, which you cannot spare?"

The woman said, "I do as all the others do, who surround me and on which I must rely on for my home, water, and my food."

Then the Lord said, "Fear the Lord![50] There is no other, But Me! For, I Am your only eternal home, and I Am your only eternal

---

[49] Mark 10:18
[50] Proverbs 15:33, 28:14

food. It was prophesied, that I Am your only eternal salvation, and only through Me, you will know that I Am the only way to Heaven for you and your children. Teach these things to your children without any added impurities or distractions of the world, and they will know Me and I will know them; and they will also inherit the Kingdom of Heaven as you show them the Way through My Love. For I have shown the whole world The True Way of The New Age through Me, as you become blood of my blood; so that others will see the True way through you to Me, just as My Mother, Mary, the Great Servant, was to her worldly husband, and to others whom you knew, served, and loved."

-- Brian Smith --

Divine Lesson: #25

The Parable of Man's Secret Treasure

There was a man who had learned of a secret treasure, the greatest of all, and the only one which he wanted or cared about. All those who had seen and heard of this treasure, said in order to find the treasure, any man must find first a secret map which allowed the man safe passage on his journey and finally he must pass through a secret door. This man questioned all whom he knew about the location of the secret treasure, the secret map, a secret passage, and the secret door but all he could learn from the tales was that he must abide in those men who knew the way created from the orders of lawmakers and oracle's who knew the answers to the secret questions but did not share their talents or ways.

The man for a while abided in the laws he was taught, and he took the tests created by the law makers who withheld the secret answers to their own accord, and after doing, he approached these who were the oracles, and they said unto him, "You have been unsuccessful in your journey to find the secret treasure. Go back to where you came from and do the same again, again, and again until you understand the secret answers so that you may gain wisdom to access to our treasure, our map, our passage and our door. For we will not give you help in your quest for wisdom, or give you compassion during your journey, nor aid you through the passage which you must cross, to open the door when you knock."

So, the man went to the Lord God in his prayers and asked His help, for the men and oracle's who lived only by their own laws-of-sin were blinded by each other and their own selves. They had no power to forgive others because they had great logs in their eyes.[51]

Then, the Lord said to the man, "Come eat at my table, knock at My door, and it shall be opened to you.[52] Your eyes will see, your ears will hear, your sins will be forgiven, and you will find the one and only treasure which you are longing for. You will learn that man on earth has not a secret map; he has not a secret passage, and no oracle's truths you will need to find which you need to know. All these who teach this are false profits. They will be caste away like dead branches which have been pruned according to their own sour deeds which I have promised. I tell you the truth, just trust and abide in Me, for the greatest treasure which you seek belongs to My father in Heaven. For I, Jesus… Am the only Way, The Truth, and the Life, and no one comes to the father, but through Me."[53]

---

[51] Matthew 7: 3-5
[52] Matthew 7: 7-8, Luke 11: 9
[53] John 14:6

-- Brian Smith --

Divine Lesson: #26

The Parable of Man's Injustice to Man

An angel, who was a patron to the church of Saint Peter, the Apostle, went to the Lord to intercede for a woman whose name he could not pronounce. He said to the Lord, "A woman we know prays to enter the Gates of Heaven too soon because she suffers much injustice completing her test?"

Then the Lord said to the angel, "Did not My Son not suffer first for her that she might not suffer so much? Did the Apostles and The Profits not suffer either? Who has suffered more, and also wished to not drink from the cup?[54] So, who among the flesh and sin is granted entrance to heaven based on lack of suffering?"

Then the angel said, "I am not the judge of these things, but You are, Oh, my Lord! I only ask because you sent me to deliver the prayers while the Holy Spirit is fighting in the arena."

God said, "It is true… He fights today, and He will win, so who will suffer most now, The Holy Spirit or the woman you represent? … Are not the cares of the Holy

---

[54] Luke 22:42

Spirit more on my plate now for the whole world, than the woman you bring forth into my shadow?"

"But this woman she weeps with a pure heart," Lord, "and she is a woman who tears will not be denied, as she cries, she is still unwed (to the Truth of The Lord's undying mercy)."

"So, what things can this woman do that continues to keep her unwed to My Truth?" Says the Lord.

"Nothing!"[55] says, the angel, "but the bent of the burden which you have given her just might make her break in the process though."

"Never!"[56] says the Lord, "For you said she is of a pure heart? So, did you not measure her heart before you came to me with this question?"

"Yes," says the angel.

"And what does this really mean?" says the Lord.

"She puts no other God nor Gods before You, and she does not use Your name in vain. She cares for the sick daily, and wears on her sleeves Thy name in righteousness. She cares only for you and none other, and bears only the symbol of your love."

"So, why do you have to ask these things if she truly is of the pure heart?" says the Lord.

"She carries one piece of baggage she can-not get rid of," says the angel.

"And what is this?" replies the Lord.

"A piece she can-not let go of. It is her connection to the world. It is her memories that hold her hostage… she is left hanging in her past."

"So, she is stuck… in her mind?" Says the Lord.

---

[55] Jeremiah 29:13
[56] I Corinthians 10:13

"Yes," says the angel, "No freedom or good medicine can she find to relieve her pain!"

"Then, you must help her see, and lead he to the gift of the Living Water so she can be baptized.[57] My Son guides her on her way," says the Lord.

So, the angel then asks, "but please, you must first command me, and then Thy Will, will be done," says the angle who was born from the seed of Peter.

The Lord God asked, "Which baggage does she hold onto which keeps her tied to Lower paradise so she can not cross over?"

"She continues to fight for justice for her neighbor's child, even unto the end," says the Lord.

"This is not her fight," says the Lord, "for I am with the Holy Spirit now as He is in the arena fighting for her as we speak . And she knows not, that He fights for her, and she is free."

"Then what should I tell her to allow her to pass over in peace?" says the angel.

"Tell her," says the Lord, "If she wishes to be greater than the Holy Spirit who fights for her today then let Gadreel keep her in her place; or she can let go and let the Holy Spirit win the battle for her which she cannot win for herself. She can look to another case also, My Son, who was also in this place, when I declared, I will make a room for you in the Inn where woman will bear a Son, and his name will be Jesus, and this child will come to save the world, and he walk where no man can walk, lest he walk

---

[57] John 4:10

-- Book of Parables II --

with me to show all the Way . And if I can do this for one, then I can do this for all."[58]

---

[58] Luke 2: 10-14

-- Brian Smith --

Divine Lesson: #27

The Parable of Man's Force of Reason

When God created man, He put in him a good force of reason which separated him from the land, and put man and his woman between the spaces of voids which God surrounded them with. On top the land in which He put them was the force of reason which made good sense, but in the space around him the force of reason made no sense. And while man walked through the land, the force of reason was on his mind, and he was in touch with the force and it touched him back and this held him captive because this was his lot from before the days of Eve. When it came to use the force of good reason an evil force came to him also to go against God, and it was a lie of reason, which is spoken to even to this day.

So, just as God created everything with the same force and breath of reason, He also created a gender force, a force of constant motion which was called binding circles where the Holy Spirit and his angels would show divine reason to protect and influence all men. For in their own world of Upper Paradise, their reason flew in circles, and in the dimensions where they watched below, The Lord God ruled over all, and all the elements, and all the dimension; So, that with justice only He could be declared all powerful and all were the same but also not the same, under Him, because they were made imperfect, and only He was perfect.

-- Book of Parables II --

In the skies, which held his breath, He made all things to be in harmony within reason; these were the waves: "The Laws" which ruled the force. He made them to live in fields of force by the right hand rule of Himself. These fields He made perfect as He was perfect, and in them, He created music, retraction, and repulsion; just as He did the same with man's soul which was destined to move either toward or away from Him, like the needle of a compass. In His waves of perfection, he created another force which could corrupt man's mind, and give glory to idols of his heart which were not made by God or by the angels. He made these to produce great fruit, with profound ideas that would bring glory to Him, and to Him alone. But man would try to decipher the waves and bring glory to himself, and this God did not tolerate.

So God said, to man, "I could have killed Satan that day in the Garden and destroyed the force between all reasons, but I did not. Why did I leave him there to be your shadow of measure? And why do you constantly tear away at the Tree of Knowledge and not give Me My Glory, and My Praise, and My Honor, and My Respect for all of that which I have created over you? Are you still so bold that you continue to play your games of hide-and-seek, and not acknowledge what I have done?" Still you believe you came from sea and not by My hand of divine order?"

And man replied, "This task to decipher lost puzzles gives my reason and then also beauty in my own eyes. I work to find no pain in my own beauty, so be it then, I will follow only my mind of reason and not my heart of chastisement?"

The God said, "Then with Satan and with temptation, by your force reason, you shall live all the days of your life in Lower Paradise with him in your command. He shall Lord over you and your offspring, bringing enmity between you and I, as you exist to choose reason, pain and suffering over Me. Satan shall put thoughts of reason into your mind to lure you in that you are greater than you truly are, and division he will create between you and your soul. I tell you the Truth, only a man who can hear what I whisper from the valleys or shout from the mountains to you today shall see the Kingdom of Heaven, and all those who do not hear will be caste away into a vacuum of no force, without reason and lost will, where there will be nothing but the gnashing of teeth, and where Satan's dark angels can-not even find you. There is where I will put you… you and your eternal chastisement which you and corrupt mind of sin and reason you so truly deserve."[59]

---

[59] Matthew 26:41

-- Book of Parables II --

Divine Lesson: #28

The Parable of The Red Cape

The angels went to the Lord and asked the Lord, "If Man is like sheep, and You are his Shepherd, and Satan is invisible to man in all things when he taunts him, then how shall man know when he, The Evil One, and his minions, are around him?"

I tell you the truth, "Man will think he is a mighty Taurus (Zeus)[60] when The Lord is absent in his prayers. He will prance like a new stud bull in the grassy fields, ready to defend his mind and soul, then give chase with his horns that only whistle in the wind. But Satan is smarter. He is like a great toreador, who has made a red cape which can-not be denied, to wave in front of man, luring him to his death as his eyes will focus only on the cape. When man chases Satan's cape, he will try to strike at it over and over, but nothing he will find there but the wind. He will chase and lunge at it, again and again, but the cape will prevail as the Evil One moves the red cape always out of reach until man become exhausted. Then Satan with his sharpened sword will run his sword into the man's heart as he lunges one last and final time. And Satan will piece his heart, cutting him into two halves so that he longer has two chambers of his heart connected into upper and lower Paradise.

---

[60] Psalm 4:2

Beware of Satan's shroud which bears his taunting cape, for it comes in many colors, shapes, forms, ideas, and desires. You must learn to run from Satan's cape, or you will be dragged away from the world's arena dead and bound by your feet, unable to walk, and be the next meal of those who lie in grassy fields ready to consume you.

This I say to you… beware of the lipstick of an impure woman, the cloth of an ungodly saint, the lure of an easy deal, the words of a false leader, and the idle time of an unwound clock. For only the pure of heart and color of the Christ's white cape is good enough for man's desires. Christ's cape will not cause him to ever fall nor stumble, and his footsteps will be true and steadfast on all terrain, while his heart be made one with the Lord in all of Paradise. He will be given untiring wings to sore like eagles and also he sings with the angels on high, and he will never have his heart cleaved in two as such nor pierced like the Son of Man, who paid the price of all man's salvation, so that any who call on his name in praise and glory will be saved from the quick and the dead."[61]

---

[61] I Peter 4

-- Book of Parables II --

Divine Lesson: #30

The Parable of The Need for Judas

When it came time for man to be enlightened before entering the gates of Heaven, the angels asked the Lord God Almighty, "What separates Man from Angels?"

He said to them, "Man must first come to know Judas, and be betrayed by him before he can know Me, so then he can learn to love unconditionally like His Father in Heaven loves him, as the angels do not." As He said this, the sun over head began to darken, the clouds began to swirl, and the earth slowed it rotation so that time stood still for just one tenth of one epoch's share.

The angels replied, "And who is Judas."[62]

The Lord God said, "Judas is the warped mirror of all the good in mankind's thoughts which turn out wrong, but knows all things before they happen. Judas is man's ability to reason and to make the choice thinking doing good is all that is needed to enter Heaven. The angels have no mirror of such. Judas made the wrong choice which lost his life and soul. He chose to reason with his mind and choose money over his heart. I myself lived beside him and with him yet he denied My Son through Me.

---

[62] Luke 22:3, John 13:27

-- Brian Smith --

I say, no man shall come to Me who denies My Son. My Son and I, our blood is one and man's blood is one with the earth. This act has but one purpose to bring my blood back to Me. And know that My suffering is enough for all. Because I have been betrayed, man must walk the same path to know and feel the similar pain I feel when I lose one of my sheep. For, I am the shepherd and the sheep know My Voice.[63] And only by listening to Judas speak in his ears, can My voice become louder, and only by Judas, will man feel his own sin.

I tell you the truth, I will separate the wheat from the chaff, the sheep from the goats, the salt from the rock, and the blood from the lamb. No one shall know me unless they know the betrayal of Judas first. Choose carefully who is to walk beside you, listen to, and follow and share your life, for the Evil One is lurking close breathing on you and giving you the same choices presented to Judas. Beware of the choices you make, and fear the Lord for He does not forget."[64]

---

[63] John 10: 27-30
[64] Matthew 25: 31-46

-- Book of Parables II --

Divine Lesson: #31

The Parable of The Bastard World

The angels asked the Lord, "Why does man choose his medals in silence, to hang on his chest with clean military favor, over claiming protection by God, and proclamation of his faith?"

Then the lord God said, "A cock crows in the night to tell all who can hear him that he wishes to rule over his hens, but also in the night a thief can come to grab him while he sleeps. The thief he knows not is like the bandit who wears a mask and has a hunger for his meat. And when he is not protected in his house, the wolf pack prays on him in the open fields, so without his cage and his silence he will lose to both the wolf and the bearer of the mask. And if he survives these two who frighten him from his roost, the silent snake who never makes a sound invades his woman's nest to eat her eggs before they hatch; for, the snake can enter any house where the cracks are small and the wire has not been drawn tight.

Then the angels asked, "How can we help protect him from the snake, the wolf, and the bandit?"

The Lord God said, "I tell you the Truth, Only the Kingdom of Heaven is secure enough from these three thieves. The walls I have built posses no hidden keys to enter its gates, and no stealth can overcome them, and there are no outer lights to find any cracks which would allow false entry. Many will come and many will try to climb them illegally, but woe to all who seek the truth too late with an impure heart, for they will be cast out and sent far away.[65]

For, do you not know the scriptures? Do you not know about Sodom and Gomorra whose walls were struck down because there were no good men inside to save? Or how, the Garden fell because a serpent found his way in to destroy a two-way love. Have not all the kingdoms on earth fallen on their own self destructive swords eventually? But my sword lives forever![66]

The world was made for lost children of sin ready to be saved. But the process is tiring for God's messengers. They were not born to live and create a ritual of song and dance for their own glory, or find Judas in the process. Oh, woe to the child who does know his Father loves him, as the Saints morn for all of them of all ages; those who cater over their offspring, for not, and those who cower over their wealth, for loss. How many more days can these children be in a bastard world and be at rest in their temporary satisfaction without delayed wisdom of gratification? All will eventually with know their doom, living a bastard life, and being separated from hope until they return to their true Father they lost, comforted in His loving arms. He is the Only -One who is good and loves them and creates them for himself, and He so longs to bring them home again, like the lost sheep that they are."[67]

---

[65] Matthew 7:22
[66] Matthew 10:24
[67] Luke 15:1-7

-- Book of Parables II --

Divine Lesson: #32

The Parable of The Lost and Found

There was a day which had no night, and a night which had no day. So, an angle on high asked the Lord as He entered the Garden for the second time, "Why have you created such a place? And for what purpose can it be?"

The Lord God answered, "Do you not know or remember the place from which you came before I created both you and man?"

"No," said the angel (while replying for the others with him), "We cannot. We have no memory of the past and all things impure past, or in the future."

The Lord God said, "Then why do you ask such a question? Is it better to know... or not to know the answer to the question which you ask? Is naivety a blessing or a curse?"

"It is better to know we believe because the answer is good...We ask because the Keeper of Souls tells us of a place which is not seen to our eyes, which lies in reserve for many who await the same, and this question is asked of us, by many who lord amongst us," said the angel.

The Lord God said to the angel, "Answer Me this and you will find out your answer that you seek, and your eyes will be opened to the future: Do you know what separates all souls from what they deserve? And why some I hold close to me and some are distant and far?"

"Love," say the angels together (all in unison)….. So, then came many more angels who came to these angel's sides (at least one hundred million or more because these were gate keepers at the walls and challengers on earth whose duty was to sit and listen); for when the word LOVE was spoken in Heaven, all angels and souls there who were sitting or lying, awoke and they came to the Lord because it was the single Call-Word which spoke the Lord's truth to the dead, and the living.

"You are correct, my good and faithful servant," said the Lord, "You that sit here beside me I love, and you also love me back. You I have found, and you have found Me back. This is the essence of day and night, and of the stars, and the Heaven, and the universe in which I placed you; and we all share in the endless time of Eternal Life."

"So why do your persist in these questions, that you also wish also to sit in and around my hands forever and never leave my side….Why, Why, Why, It is always Why?…You are not privileged like mankind yet you still ask, but have I chosen you to be the one to ask this question, which brings others to me when Love is spoken and this shakes the entrance to close to the world below."

"Love, Love, Love," sing the angels in an old hymn of praise and glory!" We know this to be true, and we repeat it on our breath, for it is the wind beneath our wings which give us flight. For You loved us from the beginning,[68] and we have loved you since the past, and we found your treat

---

[68] Isaiah 43: 18-19

lay before your door and the key that opened it wide. All of us have found it, and the saved have opened it, and we were found. It was invisible to us at first, but when we saw, we were no longer blind and when we heard, we were no longer deaf. The love you gave us was like warm water which soothed our hearts that ached for longing which was immeasurable. You measured us and each met Your measure. How great it has been for You to have shared your love, and each was found like a lost dog who needed shelter and a good master."

"You are correct, my loving angels, and the same goes for mankind who surrounds Me. Love makes you and him pure to me, and then I adore you and you adore Me. It is all about love, obedience, covenants, grace, and purity." says the Lord.

"For I cast out my sails to catch the wind like all breed of fish who are caught in a single net. I sent the Hold Spirit out like a mighty gale blowing over the earth to stir the breath of life into the dead, and collect up my breath and bring back the living. This call has gone out as Good News so that all shall hear of the treat, but only those who know the voice of the master will follow like the sheep to the shepherd. And those who cannot hear, and those who know not the voice of the shepherd, they will miss My love and I will miss them. And the place which that shall return is the place where there is not day with no night, and the place will be the same from which they were created; the place from which they came."[69]

---

[69] Mark 6:1-7

-- Brian Smith --

Divine Lesson: #33

The Parable of The Blessing, The Fruit, and The Treat

An angel asked God the Father (Creator of the son of dawn),[70] "How do you measure a man's blessing? Is it a fruit or a treat?"

There was a moment of silence, and then more silence, and then finally the Lord God spoke with only a whisper as His reply barely able to be heard, for it pained him to have to say these things, "You know how much I blessed My Son, as He did my will, and through His effort came much suffering, so He could walk His walk and find His way back to Me. Also, to My loving disciples, the Apostles, and the ones who died for their faith, I have blessed them all, as they did my will, as they endured much suffering, as they walked their walk and did not tarry and found their way back to Me. The family I chose for My Son, Jesus Christ, they too have been Blessed as they do my will, and as they suffer for Me, as they walk their walk and endure much in My name's sake as they find their way back to Me. I tell you the truth, if a man does not suffer to receive

---

[70] Isaiah 14: 12

-- Book of Parables II --

My blessing, it is but a small treat that I give him; and the treat he receives is only good for his ante; for it lies dormant like an investment which does not grow till he plays. The difference is a true Blessing grows by My will alone through great struggles and it bears much fruit in Heaven; but a treat is short lived, it vanishes like the wind, and it does not grow looking for another. My treats as I have promised will always get you to my door when I knock, but the suffered blessing which knows no end will always get you in."[71]

---

[71] I Peter 4: 12-19

-- Brian Smith --

Divine Lesson: #34

The Parable of the Tithe

Oh Malachi, Oh Malachi, Oh, where is your strength,

Why have you been burdened to lay in your tent;

Where grass does not grow and where children are sick,

While farmers are told to produce and to pitch?

Oh Malachi, Oh Malachi, are the parents naughty or nice?

Oh, tell them, their children that they are watched in the night;

For they spend all their money on gifts which all fade,

While they have little money left for the Coffers-of-Fate.

Oh Malachi, Oh Malachi, you have told of their treats,

Do they not know without suffering, there is only defeat?

Oh, Malachi, Oh Malachi, is there much left to say?

'Except to do as you do, and have none left pay.[72]

---

[72] Malachi 3:10

-- Book of Parables II --

Divine Lesson: #35

The Parable of the Wicked, the Worrisome, and the Proud

An angel came to the Lord and asked, "Over whom do you send the dark angels to watch this day? I am here to serve the mourners for the humble, and the speechless, who will have your voice and carry it in the wind?"

"The dark angels have their tools to set fires in the hearts of men, but only I have the living waters to drown the burning fires and put them out," Says the Lord. "The wicked...they burn for justice, but I am their only judge; The worrisome...they yearn for grace and mercy, but I am their only rainbow; the proud...they march in parades at the beat of their loud drums, but I am their only crusade which merits onlookers and tickertape. All these, they live in vain as the dark angels put fodder in their canons for disgust and hate, and put wheels in their hands for weight."

Then the angel said, "What must I say to those to whom you send me, that they might be saved?"

"Repent,[73] then give up all that you have and give it to the poor, then follow Me.[74] For the things of this world which matter, are not the things your eyes can see. There is

---

[73] Luke 13: 3
[74] Matthew 4:19, 8:22, 9:9, 19.21, Luke 9:23, 9:61, 14:27, 18:22

-- Brian Smith --

no light in the open cave or closed grave, only the Light in the eyes of your Master whom created the world first as your cave, and then you next after that, to toil there as your test to overcome, or perish trying!" Amen

-- Book of Parables II --

For He will command His angels
Concerning you, to guard you in all your ways;
For they will lift you up in their hands,
So that you will not strike your foot against a stone
You will tread upon the lion and the cobra;
You will trample the great lion and the serpent

Psalms 91: 11-12

www.ingramcontent.com/pod-product-compliance
Lightning Source LLC
Chambersburg PA
CBHW060858050426
42453CB00008B/1019